SHAKESPEARE'S MONOLOGUES for WOMEN

Edited by Dick Dotterer

Dramaline Publications

Library of Congress Catalog Card Number: 90-81269

Dramaline Publications
36-851 Palm View Road
Rancho Mirage, CA 92270
Phone 619/770-6076 Fax 619/770-4507

Cover design by John Sabel

This book is printed on 55# Glatfelter acid-free paper, a paper that meets the requirements of the American Standard of Permanence of paper for printed library material.

CONTENTS

INTRODUCTION

O! Those great and rewarding female roles that populate Shakespeare's world: Portia, Gertrude, Viola, Rosalind, Beatrice, Juliet, her Nurse, Lady Macbeth, Kate (the Shrew), Desdemona, Ophelia, Hermione, Imogen, Mistresses Ford and Page, Mistress Quickly, Doll Tearsheet, Lady Anne, Queen Margaret, and, of course, Cleopatra, along with a battalion of other leading and supporting roles.

Well . . . guess what?

Those ladies do not have the same quantity of great arias that their male counterparts have. And there is not a handful of soliloquies among the lot of them. This lack of great, single pieces comes as a surprise when you recall these roles in memory, or recall the impression a Shakespearean script makes on the whole. You remember great (or lousy) performances, readings, moments, scenes by various actresses. But on second reflection, the stage of your mind conjures up other characters with whom these parts share the scene. And, then, as you peruse the scripts in the supposed chronological order of their compositions, you start to see patterns and developments in Shakespeare's mastery of his craft.

The apogee of Shakespeare's craft as a playwright is his use of characters in action and in relationships in scenes to propel his story forward. A relationship requires two or more characters taking part (even soliloquies require establishment of a relationship between the characters and the audience, the listeners). After the early plays, dating ca. 1590-1594/95, Shakespeare depended less and less on grandiose recitations and more and more on sparks and conflicts in dialogue exchanges to advance the stories and develop the characters. Over-exuberant lovers, like Juliet, are bound to be verbose, but Gertrude's longest speech in *Hamlet* is her description of the death of Ophelia. Rosalind reveals herself almost totally in conversation; Viola reasons with herself only once; and Cleopatra is never alone. Finding a variety of material for an actress to work on singly from Shakespeare requires diligence, a little imagination, and some editorial gumption.

The task is made somewhat easier, however, because of the writer and the material you are working with. Shakespeare's sense of theatre is infallible, no matter which "genre" he undertakes. And "genre" in his case means comedy, tragedy, romance, and history. But his work is such a mixture and meld of types, such experimentation for his times, that the division into categories must be arbitrary and used only for simplification in discussion.

One of Shakespeare's greatest contributions to dramatic literature is that he is the first playwright since the four great Greeks to create truly female characters. And one of his influences on his contemporaries and those who came after him is to make those writers more conscious of creating more truly female characters. Compare the female characters in even his early plays with those of writers that came before him or were his early contemporaries—Kyd, Greene, Chapman, and, especially, Marlowe. Their women are stiff as redwood, ciphers, not individuals, formal statues with female names. Their women are also relatively non-influential characters in most of the stories. An actress essaying of those roles today has got to eat her Wheaties to bring one of those women to flesh and blood.

As Shakespeare became more prominent, his actors had to revel in the depth and shadings of his female characters. His contemporaries realized this achievement and they tried within their powers to emulate his achievement. Women were important to Shakespeare, both (probably) in his personal life and (definitely) in his writer's life. As an artist, he felt obligated to portray women as truly as he could.

Many of Shakespeare's ladies have a mixture of fresh and gallant ardor, a piquancy of thought, and a fortitude and bravery that could easily make them idols. We all know that Shakespeare wrote his plays for men and boys to act. Acting was a profession not fit morally for women—you could be a queen and command wars be fought and order executions, but it was immoral for a woman to appear on the public state. And Shakespeare was conscious of this same-sex convention of his theatre. His love scenes are emotionally intense and passionate, but verbal. They are physically chaste: a gesture and metaphor convey the world. From the writing, his love scenes are not intimately physical. (It was not until after women became part of the Thespian profession that directors felt the need to physicalize the scenes by more than intimation. Read the texts and see how everything is said and implied but nothing is required to be shown!) Shakespeare knew the enemies of his profession, and he was very careful not to endanger the moral reputations of his fellow actors, or engender more slander to be spread by their enemies than was being done at the time every day.

Still, all the same, Shakespeare's ladies are women. They speak with the voice of women, they think and reason with the female mind and point of view, and they feel with women's hearts and souls. Shakespeare's ladies even "soliloquize" (when they do) as women. This achievement should be considered one of the highest reaches of Shakespeare's considerable ability and one of his most important contributions to dramatic literature.

This book contains twenty-six pieces for actresses culled from nineteen of Shakespeare's plays. Most of the pieces have been constructed from a number of smaller speeches into a single, monologue scene. There are some notable Shakespearean women missing. You will not find Ophelia nor Cleopatra among these pages; nor, regrettably, Kate, Beatrice, or Lady Macbeth. Ophelia is talked to more than she talks; Cleopatra is always courted; and Kate and Beatrice are lost without their Petruchio and Benedict. The one section when Lady Macbeth is alone is not, in my opinion, either a good piece for audition nor satisfactory for a monologue scene. The material just stops. The continuation of Lady Macbeth's through-line depends on the entrance of Macbeth and their immediate interaction.

More than anything, this books should be thought of as a resource and a tool for the actress in studying acting, Shakespeare, and blank-verse. It should be thought as much a scene study book as a quick source for "classic" audition material. The pieces in this book have been consciously edited so that each of them represents a short scene, each with something for the actress to *act*. These pieces are not meant to give her merely the opportunity to recite. These pieces, with three exceptions, all involve the character talking to others in the scene, and each piece has a purpose for it being acted. These are not pieces chosen just for pretty language.

There is much to learn in handling blank-verse, and all of these pieces involve it. Blank-verse is something that is not recited in sing-song, nor is it by its very nature "naturalistic" everyday speech in delivery. It is a conscious style and requires a technique all of its own to speak it. The way it is formed in the speeches give clues as to how it should be delivered.

This book should be thought of as an acting tool. The pieces are meant for scene study or audition material. The actress should realize that some of the pieces may be too long for an audition's allotted time. She should realize that some of the speeches can be again edited to the appropriate length— especially if she knows the through-line of the speech.

The material in this book has been chosen to display the broadest contrasts and types and emotional ranges possible in Shakespeare's smorgasbord. It is arranged in the four arbitrary sections of Comedies, Tragedies, Romances, and Histories. The selections are also arranged in the order of their compositions within their various categories.

Even though this book is designed as a resource, and I have tried to give the actress something from which to build a characterization in each of the introductions, it should be self-evident that to do the pieces and the characters justice, the actress should make the time to read, and even to study, the playscript from which the piece comes. She will then know exactly where the specific piece falls within the dramatic action's build of the play and its relevancy to the play as a whole.

If an actress gives herself over to Shakespeare, she will find that his ladies offer her some of the greatest challenges and some of the most intense work she can do as an actress. But he will also present her with some of her most treasured rewards.

Part I—THE COMEDIES

THE COMEDY of ERRORS
ADRIANA—ACT II, SCENE 2

AGE: Young.   INTENT: Humorous.

Adriana is the wife of Antipholus of Ephesus. From her first appearance in the play, she is portrayed as a suspicious and jealous wife, tending toward shrewishness. On the surface, this seems to be caused by his absences and actions and wandering eye. But the roots of her suspicions and jealousies are more deeply planted than just the fear of adultery. She is unhappy with her circumstances. She wants to know why there is an inequality between the sexes—between husband and wife: "Why should their liberty than ours be more?"

On this certain day, her husband has not appeared for dinner, and his servant, Dromio of Ephesus, tells her a strange tale of being beaten by Antipholus, who has both accused his servant of stealing gold the servant has never seen and has denied having a wife. Adriana decides it's time to confront her husband, and she goes into the marketplace to search for him. She takes her sister, Luciana, with her. The two women encounter an Antipholus and a Dromio in a public place. Each man looks exactly like her husband and servant. However, they are Antipholus of Syracuse and Dromio of Syracuse, freshly arrived in Ephesus and the twins of said husband and servant. No one knows on either side of the mirror that the other set of twins exist. Adriana thinks she has found and confronted her errant and wandering husband. Antipholus of Syracuse thinks he has encountered two madwomen—and yet, perhaps, an opportunity. Mistaken identity is the fuel which powers the engine that drives the action of this play forward.

ADRIANA

Ay, ay, Antipholus, look strange and frown.
Some other mistress hath thy sweet aspects;
I am not Adriana nor thy wife.
The time was once when thou unurged wouldst vow
That never words were music to thine ear,
That never object pleasing in thine eye,
That never touch well welcome to thy hand,
That never meat sweet-savour'd in thy taste,
Unless I spake, or look'd, or touch'd, or carv'd to thee.
How comes it now, my husband, O, how comes it,
That thou art thus estranged from thyself?
Thyself I call it, being strange to me,
That, undividable, incorporate,
Am better than thy dear self's better part.
Ah, do not tear away thyself from me!
For know, my love, as easy mayst thou fall
A drop of water in the breaking gulf
And take unmingled thence that drop again,
Without addition or diminishing,
As take from me thyself and not me too.
How dearly would it touch thee to the quick,
Shouldst thou but hear I were licentious
And that this body, consecrate to thee,
By ruffian lust should be contaminate!
Wouldst thou not spit at me, and spurn at me,
And hurl the name of husband in my face,
And tear the stain'd skin off my harlot-brow,
And from my false hand cut the wedding-ring,
And break it with deep-divorcing vow?
I know thou canst, and therefore see thou do it.
I am possess'd with an adulterate blot;
My blood is mingled with the crime of lust;
For if we two be one and thou play false,
I do digest the poison of thy flesh,

Being strumpeted by thy contagion.
Keep then fair league and truce with thy true bed;
I live unstain'd, thou undishonored.

A MIDSUMMER NIGHT'S DREAM
HELENA—ACT I, SCENE I

AGE: Young.   INTENT: Humorous.

"Ay, me! . . . The course of true love never did run smooth."
    Helena has been wooed and has fallen in love with a fair
youth of Athens named Demetrius. Demetrius, however, has
passed over Helena and has now settled his intentions on
Hermia; and he has gained the consent of Hermia's father to
wed her. Hermia, however, has no interest in Demetrius for she
is in love with another Athenean youth, Lysander, who returns
her love. The more Helena loves Demetrius, the more he hates
her. The more Hermia hates Demetrius, the more he dotes on
her. When the Duke of Athens, Theseus, sides with Hermia's
father and orders her to marry Demetrius, she and Lysander
plan to elope.
    Since Hermia and Helena have been close friends since
childhood, the couple entrusts the news of their plan with her.
Helena, while gentler than Hermia, is not altogether generous.
She is in the maelstrom of unrequited love, and in this upheaval
she decides to tell Demetrius of the elopement. She hopes that
by helping him pursue Hermia, she will win Demetrius back.
    The course of true love also never did run logical.

HELENA

Call you me fair? That fair again unsay.
Demetrius loves you fair. O happy fair!
Your eyes are lodestars, and your tongue's sweet air
More tuneable than lark to shepherd's ear
When wheat is green, when hawthorn buds appear.

Sickness is catching. O, were favor so,
Yours would I catch, fair Hermia, ere I go;
My ear should catch your voice, my eye your eye,
My tongue should catch your tongue's sweet melody.
Were the world mine, Demetrius being bated,
The rest I'd give to be to you translated.
O, teach me how you look, and with what art
You sway the motion of Demetrius' heart.
       [Exit Lysander and Hermia.]
How happy some o'er other some can be!
Through Athens I am thought as fair as she.
But what of that? Demetrius thinks not so;
He will not know what all but he do know.
And as he errs, doting on Hermia's eyes,
So I, admiring of his qualities.
Things base and vile, holding no quantity,
Love can transpose to form and dignity.
Love looks not with the eyes, but with the mind,
And therefore is wing'd Cupid painted blind.
Nor hath Love's mind of any judgement taste;
Wings and no eyes, figure unheedy haste.
And therefore is Love said to be a child,
Because in choice he is so oft beguiled.
As waggish boys in game themselves forswear,
So the boy Love is perjured everywhere.
For ere Demetrius look'd on Hermia's eyne,
He hail'd down oaths that he was only mine;
And when this hail some heat from Hermia felt,
So he dissolved, and show'rs of oaths did melt.
I will go tell him of fair Hermia's flight.
Then to the wood will he tomorrow night
Pursue her; and for this intelligence
If I have thanks, it is a dear expense.
But herein mean I to enrich my pain,
To have his sight thither and back again.

A MIDSUMMER NIGHT'S DREAM
HELENA—ACT III, SCENE 2

AGE: Young.   INTENT: Humorous.

Midsummer's Eve—St. John's Eve—is a time for magic and spells. In the woods outside Athens, where Helena, Demetrius, Lysander, and Hermia are all chasing after each other, the king of the fairies, Oberon, is encamped. He has come to Athens to bless the marriage of Theseus and Hippolyta. And being in a generous mood, Oberon decides to grant Helena the love of Demetrius by enchantment. He orders his messenger, Puck, to drop the juice of a certain flower into the eyes of Demetrius, and when the youth awakes, he will dote on the first object he sees. Oberon thinks this will be Helena. Puck, however, mistakes Lysander for Demetrius, and through tried remedy to resolve the blunder, both men begin to pursue Helena through the wood, each professing his undying devotion to her. She, of course, thinks she is being mocked and ridiculed, and that all three of them—Lysander, Demetrius, and Hermia—are co-conspirators in this monstrous practical joke. Helena sees it only as a means to do her emotional injury and to deride her.

HELENA

[To Lysander and Demetrius]
O spite! O hell! I see you all are bent
To set against me for your merriment.
If you were civil and knew courtesy,
You would not do me thus much injury.
Can you not hate me, as I know you do,
But you must join in souls to mock me too?
If you were men, as men you are in show,
You would not use a gentle lady so—
To vow, and swear, and superpraise my parts,
When I am sure you hate me with your hearts.
[To Hermia.]

Now I perceive [you] have cojoin'd all three
To fashion this false sport, in spite of me.
Injurious Hermia, most ungrateful maid!
Have you conspired, have you with these contrived
To bait me with this foul derision?
Is all the counsel that we two have shared,
The sisters' vows, the hours that we have spent,
When we have chid the hasty-footed time
For parting us—O, is all forgot?
All school-days friendship, childhood innocence?
We, Hermia, like two artificial gods,
Have with our needles created both one flower,
Both on one sampler, sitting on one cushion,
Both warbling of one song, both in one key,
As if our hands, our sides, voices, and minds,
Had been incorporate. So we grew together,
Like to a double cherry, seeming parted,
But yet an union in partition;
Two lovely berries moulded on one stem;
So, with two seeming bodies, but one heart;
Two of the first, like coats in heraldry,
Due but to one and crowned with one crest.
And will you rent our ancient love asunder,
To join with men in scorning your poor friend?
It is not friendly, 'tis not maidenly.
Our sex, as well as I, may chide you for it,
Though I alone do feel the injury.
Have you not set Lysander, as in scorn,
To follow me and praise my eyes and face?
And made your other love, Demetrius,
Who even but now did spurn me with his foot,
To call me goddess, nymph, divine and rare,
Precious, celestial? Wherefore speaks he this
To her he hates? And wherefore doth Lysander
Deny your love, so rich within his soul,
And tender me, forsooth, affection,

But by your setting on, by your consent?
What though I be not so in grace as you,
So hung upon with love, so fortunate,
But miserable most, to love unloved?
This you should pity rather than despise.
Ay, do, persever, counterfeit sad looks,
Make mouths upon me when I turn my back,
Wink at each other, hold the sweet jest up.
This sport, well carried, shall be chronicled.
If you have any pity, grace, or manners,
You would not make me such an argument.
But fare ye well. 'Tis partly my own fault,
Which death, or absence, soon shall remedy.

THE MERCHANT of VENICE
PORTIA—ACT IV, SCENE 1

AGE: Young. INTENT: Serious.

Portia, heiress of Belmont, possesses beauty, wealth, and wit. She is generous, sympathetic with the less fortunate, impulsive, and ardent. She is high-spirited, intelligent, clear-sighted, noble, loyal, prompt, and decisive in action. Her sense of honor is so highly principled that she gives no hint to the lover of her choice as to which casket is the correct one to win her and her fortune—although it would mean her happiness. No wonder this girl is a prized catch, and one of the most legendary and captivating heroines in Shakespeare's canon.

Portia has secretly followed her new husband, Bassanio, back to Venice to be of what aid she can in the suit between Antonio, the merchant of Venice, and Shylock, the Jewish usurer. Portia knows that as a woman she can be of little more consequence to the trial than as moral support. But disguised as a doctor of laws (and as a man) she might be able to bring some reason to bear and influence the judgment of the ducal court.

Portia appears at the trial in the guise of Balthasar, one doctor of laws from Rome. As Balthasar, she attempts to settle the suit and save Antonio's life. At first, even in this disguise, Portia uses womanly persuasion ("The quality of mercy is not strain'd . . . ") to bring Shylock to relent on the grounds of mercy and humanity. When that approach fails to move Shylock, Portia springs the *legal trap* that makes her intellect greatly honored in the court. She sees a loophole in the deed of forfeiture which enables her to use the very law to which Shylock clings so rigidly to her advantage and, thus, to defeat Shylock's claim.

PORTIA

I pray you, let me look upon the bond.
           Why this bond is forfeit;
And lawfully by this the Jew may claim
A pound of flesh, to be by him cut off
Nearest the merchant's heart. Be merciful.
Take thrice thy money; bid me tear the bond.
           [No.] Why then, thus it is:
You must prepare your bosom for his knife.
For the intent and purpose of the law
Hath full relation to the penalty,
Which here appeareth due upon the bond.
Therefore lay bare your bosom.
Have by some surgeon, Shylock, on your charge,
To stop his wounds, lest he do bleed to death.
It is not so express'd, but what of that?
'Twere good you do so much for charity.
A pound of that same merchant's flesh is thine.
The court awards it, and the law doth give it.
And you must cut this flesh from off his breast.
The law allows it, and the court awards it.
Tarry a little; there is something else.
This bond doth give thee here no jot of blood;

The words expressly are "a pound of flesh."
Take then thy bond, take thou thy pound of flesh;
But, in the cutting it, if thou dost shed
One drop of Christian blood, thy lands and goods
Are, by the laws of Venice, confiscate
Unto the state of Venice.
                    Thyself shalt see the act;
For, as thou urgest justice, be assured
Thou shalt have justice, more than thou desir'st.
Soft!
The Jew shall have all justice. Soft, no haste.
He shall have nothing but the penalty.
Therefore prepare thee to cut off the flesh.
Shed thou no blood, nor cut thou less nor more
But just a pound of flesh; if thou tak'st more
Or less than a just pound, be it but so much
As makes it light or heavy in the substance
Or the division of the twentieth part
Of one poor scruple, nay, if the scale do turn
But in the estimation of a hair,
Thou diest, and all thy good are confiscate.
Why doth the Jew pause? Take thy forfeiture.
                    Tarry, Jew!
The law hath yet another hold on you.
It is enacted in the laws of Venice,
If it be proved against an alien
That by direct or indirect attempts
He seeks the life of any citizen,
The party 'gainst the which he doth contrive
Shall seize one half his goods; the other half
Comes to the privy coffer of the state,
And the offender's life lies in the mercy
Of the duke only, 'gainst all other voice.
In which predicament, I say, thou stand'st;
For it appears, by manifest proceeding,
That indirectly and directly too

Thou hast contrived against the very life
Of the defendant; and thou hast incurr'd
The danger formerly by me rehearsed.
Down therefore and beg mercy of the Duke.

AS YOU LIKE IT
ROSALIND—ACT III, SCENE 5

AGE: Young.   INTENT: Humorous.

As You Like It is pure comedy, with only a touch of more
serious intentions making up its foundation, like all good
comedic scripts.

The spirit of *As You Like It* is embodied in its heroine,
Rosalind. She is as fresh and exhilarating as a sunny spring
morning. Rosalind is a fountain from whose overflowing heart
life, love, and joy spurt to the world and people surrounding
her. She is sweet and affectionate, impulsive and voluble. And
she is witty, but her wit is not that which dazzles and flashes,
like, say, Beatrice's. Rosalind's wit bubbles and sparkles and
dances on the air about her.

Rosalind, the daughter of the exiled duke, has been driven
from court by her usurping uncle. She has taken refuge in the
Forest of Arden. She is accompanied by her cousin, Celia, and
the court jester, Touchstone. To escape detection, Rosalind assumes the role of a youth named Ganymede, and Celia poses as
"his" sister, Aliena. Thinking that Ganymede is really a youth,
a shepherdess named Phebe conceives a silly infatuation for
Ganymede/Rosalind, while spurning another shepherd, Silvius,
who himself yearns for Phebe.

Rosalind, Celia, and another shepherd named Corin have
come upon Phebe and Silvius, who are engaged in one of their
"courtship" fracases. Phebe diverts her immediate attention to
Ganymede/Rosalind, which Rosalind refuses to accept, and she
attempts in a firm, caustic attitude to send Phebe back into the
willing arms of Silvius.

ROSALIND

Who might be your mother,
That you insult, exult, and all at once,
Over the wretched? What though you have no beauty—
As, by my faith, I see no more in you
Than without candle may go dark to bed—
Must you be therefore proud and pitiless?
Why, what means this? Why do you look on me?
I see no more in you than in the ordinary
Of nature's sale-work. 'Od's my little life,
I think she means to tangle my eyes too!
No, faith, proud mistress, hope not after it.
'Tis not your inky brows, your black silk hair,
Your bugle eyeballs, nor your cheek of cream
That can entame my spirits to your worship.
You foolish shepherd, wherefore do you follow her,
Like foggy south, puffing with wind and rain?
You are a thousand times a properer man
Than she a woman. 'Tis such fools as you
That makes the world full of ill-favor'd children.
'Tis not her glass, but you, that flatters her,
And out of you she sees herself more proper
Than any of her lineaments can show her.
But, mistress, know yourself. Down on your knees,
And thank heaven, fasting, for a good man's love;
For I must tell you friendly in your ear,
Sell when you can, you are not for all markets.
Cry the man mercy; love him, take his offer.
Foul is most foul, being foul to be a scoffer.
So take her to thee, shepherd. Fare you well.
Come, sister. Shepherdess, look on him better,
And be not proud. Though all the world could see,
None could be so abused in sight as he.
Come, to our flock.

TWELFTH NIGHT
VIOLA—ACT II, SCENE 2

AGE: Young.   INTENT: Humorous.

Twelfth Night is the last of Shakespeare's great romantic comedies, and the last truly sunny comedy he wrote. It is also one of his brightest and most delectable. It is a play that sings with a lilt: a play filled with music and musical references, many of them wry comments on lovers' "melancholy" sighs. It is a play of gentle-folk and of a gentle life.

Viola, the play's heroine, is one of the most attractive women in all of Shakespeare's plays. She is not attractive so much for her mind or her wit—she has not the tongue nor the able quick response of her sisters Rosalind or Beatrice, nor does she have the ability to endure suffering stoically as does her cousin, Hero. No, Viola is appealing for her tender heart, her steadfast loyalty to those she loves, even at personal cost, and for the delicacy and refinement of her character.

Viola is shipwrecked and alone on the sea coast of Illyria, a stranger in a strange land, a woman who must survive. To do so, she assumes the guise of a youth, "Caesario," and obtains service as a page to a local duke, Orsino. Viola promptly falls in love with the duke. The duke, however, is pining away for the Countess Olivia, who is in mourning for her brother and is not accepting suit from anyone. Viola becomes the love-cavalier between Orsino and Olivia. Olivia, of course, swiftly becomes enamored with the handsome youth, Caesario/Viola. To ensure Caesario will return to her, Olivia sends her steward, Malvolio, after Viola to give her back her ring, which the youth/girl allegedly delivered from the duke (she did not).

Malvolio has just curtly returned the ring to Viola and has left her alone. The girl, mystified by this event, has the sudden revelation of the awkward situation in which she is finding herself—and the possible consequences of the game she must continue to play.

VIOLA

I left no ring with her. What means this lady?
Fortune forbid my outside have not charm'd her!
She made good view of me; indeed, so much,
That sure methought her eyes had lost her tongue,
For she did speak in starts distractedly.
She loves me, sure! The cunning of her passion
Invites me in this churlish messenger.
None of my lord's ring? Why, he sent her none.
I am the man. If it be so, as 'tis,
Poor lady, she were better love a dream.
Disguise, I see, thou art a wickedness.
Wherein the pregnant enemy does much.
How easy it is for the proper-false
In women's waxen hearts to set their forms!
Alas, our frailty is the cause, not we,
For such as we are made of, such we be.
How will this fadge? My master loves her dearly;
And I, poor monster, fond as much on him;
And she, mistaken, seems to dote on me.
What will become of this? As I am man,
My state is desperate for my master's love;
As I am woman—now alas the day—
What thriftless signs shall poor Olivia breathe!
O time! Thou must untangle this, not I;
It is too hard a knot for me t' untie!

ALL'S WELL that ENDS WELL
HELENA—ACT III, SCENE 2

AGE: Young.   INTENT: Serious.

Though categorized with comedies, there is little merriment in *All's Well that Ends Well*. The play is a mixture of contradictions: it sends out various signals.

Helena, too, is a catalogue of contradictions. She possesses great amiability and an indomitable inner strength. At the same time she is both clever and self-sacrificing, both meek and high-spirited, both steadfastly loyal and independent. She is willing to lose if necessary, but she is also quick to see a way to win what she desires. She appears to be a simple, straightforward, and innocent girl; yet she is firm and clear-headed about the solutions to her increasingly complicated dilemmas.

Helena is in love with Bertram, the callow, young Count of Rossillion. Her love is unrequited. Bertram has never thought of her romantically, and he considers her truly beneath him because of her parentage. Unless a miracle happens, she will never marry him.

And Helena makes the necessary miracle occur. She cures the King of his illness. As a reward, the King awards her any young man at court as her husband. She chooses Bertram. He is furious, but cannot disobey the King's command. But Bertram refuses to consummate the marriage, and he sends Helena back to his mother and his estates. Once there, she's delivered a letter from him that states, "Till I have no wife, I have nothing in France." Helena has just read this letter in the presence of the Dowager Countess and the gentlemen of the court who escorted her to Rossillion. Now, she is alone. Even at this juncture of immense rejection and hurt, Helena is willing still to make excuses for Bertram, so in love with him is she. She is willing to accept the blame for his desertion and hopes only for his safety.

HELENA

"Till I have no wife, I have nothing in France."
Nothing in France, until he has no wife!
Thou shalt have none, Rossillion, none in France;
Then hast thou all again. Poor lord, is 't I
That chase thee from thy country, and expose
Those tender limbs of thine to the event
Of the none-sparing war? And is it I
That drive thee from the sportive court, where thou
Was shot at with fair eyes, to be the mark
Of smoky muskets? O you leaden messengers,
That ride upon the violent speed of fire,
Fly with false aim; move the still-peering air
That sings with piercing; do not touch my lord.
Whoever shoots at him, I set him there;
Whoever charges on his forward breast,
I am the caitiff that do hold him to 't;
And, though I kill him not, I am the cause
His death was so effected. Better 'twere
I met the ravin lion when he roar'd
With sharp constraint of hunger; better 'twere
That all the miseries which nature owes
Were mine at once. No, come thou home, Rossillion,
Whence honor but of danger wins a scar,
As oft it loses all. I will be gone.
My being here it is that holds thee hence.
Shall I stay here to do 't? No, no, although
The air of paradise did fan the house
And angels offic'd all. I will be gone,
That pitiful rumor may report my flight
To consolate thine ear. Come, night; end, day!
For with the dark, poor thief, I'll steal away.

Part II—THE TRAGEDIES

ROMEO and JULIET
JULIET—ACT III, SCENE 2

AGE: Young.   INTENT: Serious.

Fourteen-year-old Juliet has been married to Romeo for approximately three hours. She is possessed by the rashness of her love for Romeo and by the daring and adventure of her recent act of defiance to her family: her secret marriage to the son of the family's enemy. She is exhilarated; she is impatient; she is anxious; she is euphoric; she is impetuous; she is edgy; she is eager; she is ardent. In short, she is a young girl in love and on the brink of what she thinks is a romantic adventure that ends only as she wants it to end: in eternal happiness and peace for both she and her Romeo.

Juliet is in the orchard of the Capulet house waiting for her Nurse to return with news from Romeo as to when he will see her. The scene has to be set out of doors because no room could contain the exuberance and excitement of this young girl. The walls would be forced open by her energy. She has to share with Nature what is most natural to her: the explosion of life that the love of Romeo causes in her.

JULIET

Gallop apace, you fiery-footed steeds,
Towards Phoebus' lodging! Such a wagoner
As Phaethon would whip you to the west,
And bring in cloudy night immediately.
Spread thy close curtain, love-performing night,
That runaways' eyes may wink, and Romeo
Leap to these arms, untalk'd of and unseen.
Lovers can see to do their amorous rites
By their own beauties; or, if love be blind,

It best agrees with night. Come, civil night,
Thou sober-suited matron, all in black,
And learn me how to lose a winning match,
Play'd for a pair of stainless maidenhoods.
Hood my unmann'd blood, bating in my cheeks,
With thy black mantle; till strange love grow bold,
Think true love acted simple modesty.
Come, night; come, Romeo; come, thou day in night;
For thou wilt lie upon the wings of night
Whiter than new snow on a raven's back.
Come, gentle night, come, loving, black-brow'd night,
Give me my Romeo; and, when he shall die,
Take him and cut him out in little stars,
And he will make the face of heaven so fine
That all the world will be in love with night
And pay no worship to the garish sun.
O, I have bought the mansion of a love,
But not possess'd it, and, though I am sold,
Not yet enjoy'd. So tedious is this day
As is the night before some festival
To an impatient child that hath new robes
And may not wear them. O, here comes my nurse,
And she brings news; and every tongue that speaks
But Romeo's name speaks heavenly eloquence.

ROMEO and JULIET
JULIET—ACT III, SCENE 2

AGE: Young.   INTENT: Serious.

How quickly euphoria turns to calamity. The Nurse has returned with the news of Romeo for Juliet, but not the news that
she expected. The Nurse tells Juliet of Tybalt's death at
Romeo's hands. At first Juliet thinks it is Romeo who is slain,
and her world collapses. And then, when she sorts out the truth,
she reviles Romeo for killing her beloved cousin (and now his

kinsman, too). When the Nurse, in her grief, again berates Romeo for his revenge on the death of Mercutio, Juliet switches emotions again and upbraids the Nurse for maligning Romeo.

JULIET

Blister'd be thy tongue
For such a wish! He was not born to shame.
Upon his brow shame is ashamed to sit;
For 'tis a throne where honor may be crown'd
Sole monarch of the universal earth.
O, what a beast was I to chide at him!
Shall I speak ill of him that is my husband?
Ah, poor my lord, what tongue shall smooth thy name
When I, thy three-hours wife, have mangled it?
But, wherefore, villain, didst thou kill my cousin?
That villain cousin would have killed my husband.
Back, foolish tears, back to your native spring;
Your tributary drops belong to woe,
Which you, mistaking, offer up to joy.
My husband lives, that Tybalt would have slain,
And Tybalt's dead, that would have slain my husband.
All this is comfort. Wherefore weep I then?
Some word there was, worser than Tybalt's death,
That murder'd me. I would forget it fain,
But, O, it presses to my memory
Like damned guilty deeds to sinners' minds:
"Tybalt is dead, and Romeo—banished."
That 'banished,' that one word 'banished,'
Hath slain ten thousand Tybalts. Tybalt's death
Was woe enough, if it had ended there;
Or, if sour woe delights in fellowship
And needly will be rank'd with other griefs,
Why follow'd not, when she said "Tybalt's dead,"
Thy father, of thy mother, nay, or both,

Which modern lamentation might have moved?
But with the rearward following Tybalt's death,
"Romeo is banished," to speak that word,
Is father, mother, Tybalt, Romeo, Juliet,
All slain, all dead. "Romeo is banished!"
There is no end, no limit, measure, bound,
In that word's death; no words can that woe sound.
O, find him! Give this ring to my true knight,
And bid him come to take his last farewell.

JULIUS CAESAR
PORTIA—ACT II, SCENE 1

AGE: Any age.   INTENT: Serious.

Portia, wife of Brutus, the play's presumptive hero, is one of
the only two women in *Julius Caesar*; Calpurnia, Caesar's
wife, is the other. Portia has but two scenes, and in the first one
Shakespeare compacts the life, loves, worries, hopes, and fortitude of this noble woman.

Brutus has been approached by Cassius and a group of conspirators to join with them in the planned assassination of
Caesar. (The conspirators need Brutus' participation to add a
legitimate gloss to their mealy plan.) Whereas before in their
marriage Brutus has always confided and consulted with Portia,
this time he keeps her at an emotional distance, and he also
keeps his own counsel. Portia has absorbed in silence as much
of this uncharacteristic behavior of her husband as she can
bear, but now Brutus has left their bed chamber in the middle
of an unruly night to roam in the orchard. Portia, hurt by his
actions and the closure of himself from her, confronts him.

PORTIA

Brutus, my lord! You've ungently, Brutus,
Stole from my bed. And yesternight, at supper,
You suddenly arose, and walk'd about,
Musing and sighing, with your arms across,
And when I ask'd you what the matter was,
You stared upon me with ungentle looks.
I urged you further; then you scratch'd your head,
And too impatiently stamp'd with your foot.
Yet I insisted, yet you answer'd not,
But, with and angry wafture of your hand,
Gave sign for me to leave you. So I did,
Fearing to strengthen that impatience
Which seem'd too much enkindled, and withal
Hoping it was but an effect of humor,
Which sometime hath his hour with every man.
It will not let you eat, nor talk, nor sleep,
And could it work so much on your shape
As it hath much prevail'd on your condition,
I should not know you, Brutus. Dear my lord,
Make me acquainted with your cause of grief.
Is Brutus sick? And is it physical
To walk unbraced and suck up the humors
Of the dank morning? What, is Brutus sick,
And will he steal out of his wholesome bed
To dare the vile contagion of the night,
And tempt the rheumy and unpurged air
To add unto his sickness? No, my Brutus,
You have some sick offense within your mind,
Which, by the right and virtue of my place,
I ought to know of. And, upon my knees,
I charm you, by my once-commended beauty,
By all your vows of love, and that great vow
Which did incorporate and make us one,
That you unfold to me, yourself, your half,

Why are you heavy, and what men tonight
Have had resort to you, for here have been
Some six or seven, who did hide their faces
Ever from darkness.
Within the bond of marriage, tell me, Brutus,
Is it excepted I should know no secrets
That appertain to you? Am I yourself
But, as it were, in sort of limitation,
To keep you at meals, comfort your bed,
And talk to you sometimes? Dwell I but in the suburbs
Of your good pleasure? If it be no more,
Portia is Brutus' harlot, not his wife.

HAMLET
QUEEN GERTRUDE—ACT IV, SCENE 7

AGE: Mature.   INTENT: Serious.

Personal sorrows mount close upon new calamities in the troubled kingdom of Denmark. Laertes has recently returned from France to learn that his father, Polonius, was killed by Prince Hamlet, who had gotten away scot-free for doing it; that Polonius, to add insult to injury, was not buried honorably with the heraldic ceremony due his position; and, finally, he finds his sister, Ophelia, has lost her sanity.

Claudius and his queen, Gertrude, work together in their most personal and political collaboration to keep Laertes under control and to prevent him from murderous outbursts. These outbursts especially concern Gertrude because they are aimed against both her husband and her son. Just as it seems that Claudius has managed to allay Laertes, Gertrude brings the news that Ophelia has drowned. The queen gives her detailed description of the death of Ophelia in reply to Laertes' anguished "Drown'd! O, where?" This comes from his deep-rooted need to know what and where it happened, and to be taken to his sister.

The Queen's main objective is to assuage Laertes' anxieties and to keep him from renewing his murderous impulses. Her detailed description is not a ghoulish recounting, but a means to convince Laertes that Ophelia's death was an *accident*. Her intention is to convince Laertes that Ophelia went to her death with no terror and that she never actually realized the danger she was in.

It is interesting that the Queen's recitation is that of an observer who might, from a distance, interpret the witnessed scene in just such a manner, while one who overhears the tale might interpret the act in a completely different way—as happens later in the play.

QUEEN GERTRUDE

One woe doth tread upon another's heel,
So fast they follow. Your sister's drown'd, Laertes.
There is a willow grows askant the brook,
That shows his hoar leaves in the glassy stream;
Therewith fantastic garlands did she make
Of crow-flowers, nettles, daisies, and long purples
That liberal shepherds give a grosser name,
But our cold maids do dead men's fingers call them.
There, on the pendent boughs her cronet weeds
Clamb'ring to hang, an envious sliver broke,
When down her weedy trophies and herself
Fell in the weeping brook. Her clothes spread wide,
And, mermaid-like, awhile they bore her up,
Which time she chanted snatches of old hymns;
As one incapable of her own distress,
Or like a creature native and indued
Unto that element. But long it could not be
Till that her garments, heavy with their drink,
Pull'd the poor wretch from her melodious lay
To muddy death.
Drown'd, drown'd.

OTHELLO
DESDEMONA—ACT I, SCENE 3

AGE: Young.   INTENT: Serious.

Desdemona has always been hailed as the sacrificial victim of both Othello and Iago, "a victim consecrated from the first," as one 19th century commentator wrote. But Desdemona does not know she is a victim, nor does she see herself as a potential one until near the conclusion of her story. Desdemona is, in fact, like so many of Shakespeare's women, very brave and piquantly outspoken in her innocence.

Like Juliet, Desdemona is rash in her love for Othello. In 16th century terms, it was a very grievous fault for a daughter to marry without her father's knowledge or consent. Brabantio, her father, thinks Desdemona was gulled into marriage by witchcraft, has forced Othello before the Duke of Venice at sword's point. At Othello's request, the Duke summons Desdemona to give testimony on Othello's behalf—or to refute him. Desdemona, with natural gentleness and refined grace, defies both her family and the conventional attitude of Venice. She is, indeed, a brave young woman.

DESDEMONA

My noble father,
I do perceive here a divided duty.
To you I am bound for life and education;
My life and education both do learn me
How to respect you. You are the lord of duty;
I am hitherto your daughter. But here's my husband,
And so much duty as my mother show'd
To you, preferring you before her father,
So much I challenge that I may profess
Due to the Moor my lord.
Most gracious Duke,

To my unfolding lend your prosperous ear,
And let me find a charter in your voice
T' assist my simpleness.
That I did love the Moor to live with him,
My downright violence and storm of fortunes
May trumpet to the world. My heart's subdued
Even to the very quality of my lord.
I saw Othello's visage in his mind,
And to his honors and valiant parts
Did my soul and fortunes consecrate.
So that, dear lords, if I be left behind,
A moth of peace, and he go to the war,
The rites for which I love him are bereft me,
And I a heavy interim shall support
By his dear absence. Let me go with him.

OTHELLO
DESDEMONA—ACT III, SCENE 4

AGE: Young.   INTENT: Serious.

On the island of Cyprus, away from family and familiar
friends, Desdemona is ripe for her sacrificial role in Iago's
treachery toward Othello. At this point, Desdemona still views
Iago as a loyal and reliable friend, though, perhaps, tactless, but
dependable. This works to Iago's advantage. Everyone falls
into his pocket, and no one seems the wiser to what he is doing.
Iago has started his workings on Othello's trusting mind; he
has assured that his wife, Emilia, will work on Desdemona to
intercede with Othello on behalf of Cassio; and he has
convinced Cassio that he should ask Desdemona for her help in
regaining his place in both Othello's esteem and military ranks.
Desdemona, who has an even more trusting soul than does
Othello, is fully swept into the intrigue, as so many innocents
are, by viewing everyone else's motives in light of her own
blameless ones.

Cassio and Emilia have joined Desdemona in the Cypriot castle, and Desdemona is assuring Cassio that she will intervene with Othello on his behalf.

DESDEMONA

        Alas, thrice-gentle Cassio!
My advocation is not now in tune.
My lord is not my lord; nor should I know him,
Were he in favor as in humor alter'd.
So help me every spirit sanctified,
As I have spoken for you all my best
And stood within the blank of his displeasure
For my free speech! You must awhile be patient.
What I can do I will, and more I will
Than for myself I dare. Let that suffice you.
        Something, sure, of state,
Either from Venice, or some unhatch'd practice
Made demonstrable here in Cyprus to him,
Hath puddled his clear spirit; and in such cases
Men's natures wrangle with inferior things,
Though great ones are their object. 'Tis even so;
For let our finger ache, and it endues
Our other healthful members even to a sense
Of pain. Nay, we must think men are not gods,
Nor of them look for such observancy
As fits the bridal. Beshrew me much, Emilia,
I was, unhandsome warrior as I am,
Arraigning his unkindness with my soul;
But now I find I had suborn'd the witness,
And he's indicted falsely.
I will go seek him. Cassio, walk here about.
If I do find him fit, I'll move your suit
And seek to effect it to my uttermost.

Part III—THE ROMANCES

PERICLES
DIONYZA—ACT IV, SCENE 1

AGE: Mature (Any age).   INTENT: Serious.

Dionyza is the wife to Cleon, the governor of the City of
Tarsus. Early in his adventures, Pericles brings shiploads of re-
lief goods to the suffering city, and he earns the gratitude of
Cleon and Dionyza for his charity. Later, when Pericles
believes his wife has died in childbirth aboard ship and has
been buried at sea, he fosters his baby daughter, Marina, onto
Cleon and Dionyza. He charges that they raise the baby with
"princely training, that she may be/Manner'd as she born."

Marina is raised side by side with Dionyza's own daughter,
Philoten. Both girls blossom, but Marina's blossoms are
brighter and sweeter. While this doesn't seem to bother
Philoten, it causes "rare envy" in Dionyza, who feels the
virtues of her own daughter are being obscured by the abilities
and traits of Marina. Dionyza decides, therefore, that the only
way for Philoten to "stand peerless" against Marina is to have
Marina murdered.

At this moment, Dionyza is walking along the open space
near the seashore with her servant, Leonine, whom she has paid
to become a murderer. Dionyza gives him final encouragement
on how safe it is to kill Marina without being detected and
warns him not to let his conscience get in his way. Propitiously,
Marina, who has been out picking flowers, crosses their path
and gives Dionyza and Leonine their opportunity immediately.

DIONYZA

[To Leonine.]
Thy oath remember; thou has sworn to do 't:
'Tis but a blow, which never shall be known.

Thou canst not do a thing in the world so soon,
To yield thee so much profit. Let not conscience,
Which is but cold, inflaming love i' thy bosom,
Inflame too nicely; nor let pity, which
Even women have cast off, melt thee, but be
A soldier to thy purpose.
Here she comes weeping for her nurse's death. Thou
art resolved? . . .
   [Enter Marina, with a basket of flowers.]
How now, Marina! Why do you keep alone?
How chance my daughter is not with you? Do not
Consume your blood with sorrowing; you have
A nurse of me. Lord, how your favor's changed
With this unprofitable woe!
Come, give me your flowers, ere the sea mar it.
Walk with Leonine; the air is quick there,
And it pierces and sharpens the stomach. Come,
Leonine, take her by the arm, walk with her.
      Come, come;
I love the King your father, and yourself,
With more than foreign heart. We every day
Expect him here. When he shall come and find
Our paragon to all reports thus blasted,
He will repent the breadth of his great voyage,
Blame both my lord and me that we have taken
No care to your best courses. Go, I pray you,
Walk, and be cheerful once again. Reserve
That excellent complexion, which did steal
The eyes of young and old. Care not for me;
I can go home alone.
Come, come, I know 'tis good for you.
Walk half an hour, Leonine, at the least.
Remember what I have said. [Exit.]

CYMBELINE
THE QUEEN—ACT I, SCENE 5

AGE: Mature (Any age).   INTENT: Serious.

Cymbeline's Queen could serve as the mentor for Cinderella's grasping stepmother or the wicked queen in *Snow White*. Those two infamous, better-known ladies are, in fact, pale imitations of this Queen.

    Cymbeline is an odd play. It is a mixture of romance and folklore, tragicomedy, melodrama, heroic epic, morality; and an exploration of loyalty and devotion, betrayal and deceit, truth triumphant, and love's power to forgive. It is an experimental play, more ponderous than inspired, and like so many trial experiments into untravelled realms, one that never quite makes up its mind what kind of play it wants to be. Perhaps it is kindest to say that it's a notebook of ideas, some of which are brought to fulfillment in the two masterpieces that followed it: *The Winter's Tale* and *The Tempest*.

    The Queen is at least Cymbeline's second wife and she has complete ascendancy over him. By his first wife, Cymbeline had two sons and a daughter. The two sons are thought long dead, so his daughter, Imogen, is the heir presumptive to the kingdom. The queen wants her son by a previous marriage, who is an oaf of the first rank, to succeed to the throne. To do that, however, Cloton (her son), needs to marry Imogen. Imogen not only spurns Cloton, but she also marries Posthumus Leonatius against her father's wishes.

    The Queen hates Imogen for rejecting Cloton. While pretending to support Imogen, she goads Cymbeline to further punishment for the couple. The Queen is crafty, able, and totally unscrupulous.

    Just at the moment before, the Queen has received from a compromised doctor a casket of poisons which she intends to deliver to Imogen. The Queen cannot appear to be involved in Imogen's murder, and she knows it. To this end, she has sent for Pisanio, servant to Posthumus and loyal to Imogen. She intends him to be the unknowing messenger of Imogen's death.

QUEEN

[Enter Pisanio.]
[Aside.] Here comes a flattering rascal; upon him
Will I first work. He's for his master,
And enemy to my son. How now, Pisanio!
       Hark thee, a word.
Weeps she still, say'st thou? Dost thou think in time
She will not quench and let instructions enter
Where folly now possesses? Do thou work.
When thou shalt bring me word she loves my son,
I'll tell thee on the instant thou art then
As great as is thy master; greater, for
His fortunes all lie speechless and his name
Is at last gasp. Return he cannot, nor
Continue where he is. To shift his being
Is to exchange one misery with another,
And every day that comes comes to decay
A day's work in him. What shalt thou expect
To be depender on a thing that leans,
Who cannot be new built, nor has no friends,
So much as but to prop him?
   [The Queen drops the box: Pisanio takes it up.]
       Thou tak'st up
Thou know'st not what; but take it for thy labor.
It is a thing I made, which hath the King
Five times redeem'd from death. I do not know
What is more cordial. Nay, I prithee, take it;
It is an earnest of a farther good
That I mean to thee. Tell thy mistress how
The case stands with her; do 't as from thyself.
Think what a chance thou changest on, but think
Thou hast thy mistress still—to boot, my son,

Who shall take notice of thee. I'll move the king
To any shape of thy preferment such
As thou 'lt desire; and then myself, I chiefly,
That set thee on to this desert, am bound
To load thy merit richly. Fare thee well, Pisanio;
Think on my words. [Exit Pisanio.]
        A sly and constant knave,
Not to be shaked; the agent for his master
And the remembrancer of her to hold
The hand-fast to her lord. I have given him that
Which, if he take, shall quite unpeople her
Of liegers for her sweet, and which she after,
Except she bend her humor, shall be assured
To taste of too.

CYMBELINE
IMOGEN—ACT III, SCENE 2

AGE: Young.   INTENT: Serious.

Imogen is the only daughter and last surviving child of
Cymbeline, a king of ancient Britain. She is also a much put-
upon lady, and through it all she remains gentle, beautiful,
steadfast, and, of course, innocent. Throughout her trials, she
retains her fortitude and her grace, and, in the end, she
blossoms with magnanimity toward all. Imogene is also a
young woman with feelings and ideas of her own. Among
those ideas is that she should be allowed to follow her heart
and be able to marry whom she chooses for love and not for
reasons of state, business, or practicality to benefit others in her
family. Imogen marries a "worthy, but poor gentleman" who is
not of her class, and by doing so incurs the wrath of her father.
    The King exiles Posthumus, and to his mind the marriage is
ended. Imogen, however, does not accept it, and in far-off
Rome, neither does Posthumus. So sure is Posthumus of his lady's fidelity that he makes an absurd bet with a new acquain-

tance, an Italian named Iachimo. Iachimo bets Posthumus that he can bed the virtuous Imogen. (Iachimo is a cad and scoundrel who is worthy of mention in the same breath as some of Shakespeare's other unscrupulous opportunists—Italian or otherwise.)

Imogen of course spurns Iachimo. But Iachimo gains access to Imogen's bedchamber through a "trunk trick." Back in Rome, Iachimo presents Posthumus with his "proof" of his successful seduction: a bracelet he has stolen off the arm of the sleeping Imogen, plus a description of her chamber, as well as knowledge of a certain part of her hidden anatomy. Posthumus has no reason to doubt Iachimo's veracity and Imogen's infidelity.

Posthumus' pride is wounded to oceanic depths. He is betrayed and wants revenge. To this end, he writes two letters: an obsequious one to Imogen to lure her from the palace and to meet him clandestinely at Milford-Haven in Wales. The second letter is to the loyal Pisanio. This letter makes the accusation of adultery and orders Pisanio to kill Imogen once they arrive at Milford-Haven.

Imogen has just received the letter intended for her from her sorely missed Posthumus. Here is a young bride and wife whose deepest wish is about to be fulfilled.

IMOGEN

[Reads] "Justice, and your father's wrath, should he take me in his dominion, could not be so cruel to me, as you, O the dearest of creatures, would even renew me with your eyes. Take notice that I am in Cambria, at Milford-Haven. What your own love will out of this advise you, follow. So he wishes you all happiness that remains loyal to his vow, and your increasing in love. Leonatus Posthumus."
O, for a horse with wings! Hear'st thou Pisanio?
He is at Milford-Haven. Read, and tell me
How far 'tis thither. If one of mean affairs

May plot it in a week, why may not I
Glide thither in a day? Then, true Pisanio,
Who long'st, like me, to see thy lord; who long'st—
O, let me bate—but not like me, yet long'st,
But in a fainter kind—O, not like me,
For mine's beyond beyond, say, and speak thick—
Love's counselor should fill the bores of hearing,
To the smothering of the sense—how far it is
To this same blessed Milford. And by the way,
Tell me how Wales was made so happy as
To inherit such a haven. But first of all,
How we may steal from hence, and for the gap
That we shall make in time from our hence-going
And our return, to excuse. But first, how get hence?
Why should excuse be born or ere begot?
We'll talk of that hereafter. Prithee, speak,
How many score of miles may we well rid
'Twixt hour and hour?
Go bid my woman feign a sickness, say
She'll home to her father; and provide me presently
A riding-suit, no costlier than would fit
A franklin's housewife.
I see before me, man. Nor here, nor here,
Nor what ensues, but have a fog in them,
That I cannot look through. Away, I prithee!
Do as I bid thee. There's no more to say.
Accessible is none but Milford way.

CYMBELINE
IMOGEN—ACT III, SCENE 4

AGE: Young.   INTENT: Serious.

Two scenes later in the play, Imogen and Pisanio arrive at Milford-Haven. Pisanio knows that his master is wrong and that his mistress is innocent of any wrongdoing. He will not murder the girl, and he shows Imogen the letter Posthumus sent him and the real reason for their journey to Wales.

The contrast between Imogen's emotional reactions to this second letter and her reactions to the first help define the complexity and breadth of emotional range and traumatic situations which Imogen traverses throughout the play. It is in such extremes that Shakespeare creates a character that for an actress is both striking and interesting: challenge to be both bold and human at the same time.

IMOGEN

[Reads] "Thy mistress, Pisanio, hath played the strumpet in my bed; the testimonies whereof lie bleeding in me. I speak not out of weak surmises, but from proof as strong as my grief and as certain as I expect my revenge. That part thou, Pisanio, must act for me, if thy faith be not tainted with the breach of hers. Let thine own hands take away her life. I shall give thee opportunity at Milford-Haven—he hath my letter for the purpose—where, if thou fear to strike and to make me certain it is done, thou art the pandar to her dishonor and equally to me disloyal."
False this to bed! What is it to be false?
To lie in watch there and to think on him?
To weep 'twixt clock and clock? If sleep charge nature,
To break it with a fearful dream of him
And cry myself awake? That's false to 's bed, is it?
I false! Thy conscience witness! Iachimo,
Thou didst accuse him of incontinency;

Thou then look'dst like a villain; now methinks
Thy favor's good enough. Some jay of Italy,
Whose mother was her painting, hath betray'd him:
Poor I am stale, a garment out of fashion,
And, for I am richer than to hang by the walls,
I must be ripp'd. To pieces with me! O,
Men's vows are women's traitors! All good seeming,
By thy revolt, O husband, shall be thought
Put on for villainy; not born where 't grows,
But worn a bait for ladies.
True honest men being heard, like false Aeneas,
Were in his time thought false, and Sinon's weeping
Did scandal many a holy tear, took pity
From most true wretchedness. So thou, Posthumus,
Wilt lay the leaven on all proper men;
Goodly and gallant shall be false and perjured
From thy great fail. Come, fellow, be thou honest;
Do thou thy master's bidding. When thou see'st him,
A little witness my obedience. Look!
I draw the sword myself. Take it, and hit
The innocent mansion of my love, my heart.
Fear not; 'tis empty of all things but grief.
Thy master is not there, who was indeed
The riches of it. Do his bidding; strike.
Thou mayst be valiant in a better cause,
But now thou seem'st a coward.
        Why, I must die;
And if I do not by thy hand, thou art
No servant of thy master's. Against self-slaughter
There is prohibition so divine
That cravens my weak hand. Come, here's my heart.
Something's afore 't. Soft, soft! We'll no defense;
Obedient as the scabbard. What is here?
The scriptures of the loyal Leonatus,
All turn'd to heresy? Away, away,
Corrupters of my faith! You shall no more

Be stomachers to my heart. Thus may poor fools
Believe false teachers. Though those that are betray'd
Do feel the treason sharply, yet the traitor
Stands in worse case of woe.
And thou, Posthumus, thou that didst set up
My disobedience 'gainst the King my father
And make me put into contempt the suits
Of princely fellows, shalt hereafter find
It is no act of common passage, but
A strain of rareness: and I grieve myself
To think, when thou shalt be disedged by her
That now thou tirest on, how thy memory
Will then be pang'd by me. Prithee, dispatch.
The lamb entreats the butcher.

THE TEMPEST
MIRANDA—ACT III, SCENE 1

AGE: Young.   INTENT: Serious.

Miranda was only three or four years old when she was cast-
away on a strange, enchanted, uncharted island with her father.
For twelve years she has had no human contact save for her father, the austere sorcerer Prospero, and the deformed, savage
inhabitant of the island, Caliban, who is her father's slave.
Prospero has been her only teacher and her only source of society. Her views have tended to reflect his until this one fateful
day when she experiences a "brave new world." A shipload of
men are tossed ashore by a violent sea tempest—all engineered
by Prospero and his magic.
    The first human Miranda sees since she was a child too
young to remember them is the young prince of Naples,
Ferdinand. And, as in all fairy tales controlled by magic, it is
love at first sight between them. But Prospero has other plans
"lest too light winning/Make the prize light." He orders
Miranda not to speak to the young stranger, and he causes

Ferdinand to labor in his service. Love, however, is too strong for Miranda to obey her father. She knows her father's habits— she knows when he will be otherwise occupied—and she waits for that opportunity to speak to Ferdinand. Being "unconventional" (by the rules of another's society), Miranda does not hesitate to say openly what she thinks or feels to Ferdinand.

MIRANDA

Alas, now, pray you,
Work not so hard. I would the lightning had
Burnt up those logs you are enjoin'd to pile!
Pray, set it down and rest you. When this burns,
'Twill weep for having wearied you. My father
Is hard at study; pray now, rest yourself.
He's safe for these three hours. If you'll sit down,
I'll bear your logs the while. Pray, give me that.
I'll carry it to the pile. It would become me
As well as it does you; and I should do it
With much more ease, for my good will is to it,
And yours it is against. You look wearily.
          I do not know
One of my sex; no woman's face remember,
Save, from my glass, mine own. Nor have I seen
More that I may call men than you, good friend,
And my dear father. How features are abroad,
I am skilless of; but, by my modesty,
The jewel in my dower, I would not wish
Any companion in the world but you,
Nor can imagination form a shape,
Besides yourself, to like of. But I prattle
Something too wildly, and my father's precepts
I therein do forget. Do you love me?
          I am a fool
To weep at what I am glad of. [I weep]

At mine unworthiness, that dare not offer
What I desire to give, and much less take
What I shall die to want. But this is trifling,
And all the more it seeks to hide itself,
The bigger bulk it shows. Hence, bashful cunning,
And prompt me, plain and holy innocence!
I am your wife, if you will marry me;
If not, I'll die your maid. To be your fellow
You may deny me, but I'll be your servant,
Whether you will or no. My husband, then?
[My hand,] with my heart in 't. And now farewell
Till half an hour hence.

Part IV—THE HISTORIES

KING HENRY VI, PART II
QUEEN MARGARET—ACT III, SCENE 2

AGE: Young [Any age].   INTENT: Serious.

The first great, legendary female character from William
Shakespeare's pen is Margaret of Anjou, queen to the saintly
and imbecilic King Henry VI. She appears first in Act V, Scene
3 of *King Henry VI, Part I*; then she is the dominant female
character in both *King Henry VI, Parts II & III*; and she sums
up her career as the dramatically effective "Cassandra," the
mad, deposed Queen Margaret, in *King Richard III*.

Shakespeare's Queen Margaret is coarse, fierce, revengeful,
and unprincipled. And above all, she is strong. She has to be,
for not only is Henry VI a weak king, he is also a hopeless one;
and Margaret is trying to hold the kingdom together and the
throne for the Lancasterian dynasty. Added to this, she is not in
love with her husband but with the handsome and audacious
Duke of Suffolk, who negotiated her marriage. During her long
reign as queen-consort, Margaret managed to raise armies, lead
them to victory and disaster, offend her nobility and her allies,
and to lose the throne not once but twice. She knew how to
make solid enemies.

Among the early enemies was the Duke of Gloucester, uncle
to King Henry. Suffolk arranges the murder of Gloucester, and
he then brings the news to the King at Bury St. Edmunds, before the whole court. The King faints at the news, and when
Suffolk and the Queen try to comfort him, the King recoils
from them in a mad outburst. The Queen is stung by the King's
accusation that she is treacherous toward him, or that she was
involved in Gloucester's death. She reacts immediately,
passionately, and violently—and perhaps just a bit too
zealously—in her defense of both herself and Suffolk.

QUEEN MARGARET

Why do you rate my Lord of Suffolk thus?
Although the Duke was enemy to him,
Yet he most Christian-like laments his death.
And for myself, foe as he was to me,
Might liquid tears of heart-offending groans
Or blood-consuming sighs recall his life,
I would be blind with weeping, sick with groans,
Look pale as primrose with blood-drinking sighs,
And all to have the noble Duke alive.
What know I how the world may deem of me?
For it is known we were but hollow friends.
It may be judged I made the Duke away;
So shall my name with slander's tongue be wounded,
And princes' courts be fill'd with my reproach.
This get I by his death. Ay me, unhappy!
To be a queen, and crown'd with infamy!
Be woe for me, more wretched than he is.
What, dost thou turn away and hide thy face?
I am no loathsome leper. Look on me.
What! Art thou, like the adder, waxen deaf?
Be poisonous too, and kill thy forlorn queen.
Is all thy comfort shut in Gloucester's tomb?
Why, then, dame Margaret was ne'er thy joy.
Erect his statue and worship it,
And make my image but an alehouse sign.
Was I for this nigh wrack'd upon the sea
And twice by awkward wind from England's bank
Drove back again unto my native clime?
What boded this, but well forewarning wind
Did seem to say, "Seek not a scorpion's nest,
Nor set no footing on this unkind shore"?
What did I then but cursed the gentle gusts
And he that loos'd them forth their brazen caves,
And bid them blow towards England's blessed shore,

Or turn our stern upon a dreadful rock?
Yet Aeolus would not be a murderer,
But left that hateful office unto thee.
The pretty-vaulting sea refused to drown me,
Knowing that thou wouldst have me drown'd on shore
With tears as salt as sea, through thy unkindness.
The splitting rocks cowr'd in the sinking sands
And would not dash me with their ragged sides,
Because thy flinty heart, more hard than they,
Might in thy palace perish Margaret.
As far as I could ken thy chalky cliffs,
When from thy shore the tempest beat us back,
I stood upon the hatches in the storm,
And when the dusky sky began to rob
My earnest-gaping sight of thy land's view,
I took a costly jewel from my neck—
A heart it was, bound in with diamonds—
And threw it towards thy land. The sea received it,
And so I wish'd thy body might my heart.
And even with this I lost fair England's view
And bid mine eyes be packing with my heart
And call'd them blind and dusky spectacles,
For losing ken of Albion's wished coast.
How often have I tempted Suffolk's tongue,
The agent of thy foul inconstancy,
To sit and witch me, as Ascanius did
When he to madding Dido would unfold
His father's acts commenced in burning Troy!
Am I not witch'd like her, or thou not false like him?
Ay me, I can no more! Die, Margaret!
For Henry weeps that thou dost live so long.

KING HENRY VI, PART III
QUEEN MARGARET—ACT V, SCENE 4

AGE: Mature [Any age].   INTENT: Serious.

The Lancasterian forces have nearly lost The War of the Roses. King Henry is deposed, and the Yorkist heir, Edward, has been crowned King Edward IV. But Margaret and her son, Edward, Prince of Wales, are still in the field. They have, however, recently lost one of the last two decisive battles of the War, the Battle of Barnet, and they are now about to engage in the last battle, the final Yorkist triumph, the Battle of Tewksbury.

The Lancasterian cause is all but over, and their forces are humiliated. This is their last-ditch stand. Margaret is in the field with her son and the remains of the nobles and forces still loyal to her. Shakespeare has been very careful in his lengthy portrayal of Margaret: she remains consistant throughout all of the plays, as she is described in this one: "O tiger's heart wrapped in a woman's hide!" She is also motivated by the chief theme of this play: revenge. She does not want just to win, she does not want simply heavenly justice: everything she does is motivated by "Revenge!" (She also knows what lies in store for them if they lose this battle and are captured alive after it.) This is her final attempt to stir her nobles' blood and arouse them for battle—a battle they cannot lose.

QUEEN MARGARET

Great lords, wise men ne'er sit and wail their loss,
But cheerly seek how to redress their harms.
What though the mast be now blown overboard,
The cable broke, the holding-anchor lost,
And half our sailors swallow'd in the flood?
Yet lives our pilot still. Is 't meet that he
Should leave the helm and, like a fearful lad,
With tearful eyes add water to the sea,

And give more strength to that which hath too much,
Whiles, in his moan, the ship splits on the rock,
Which industry and courage might have saved?
Ah, what shame, ah, what a fault were this!
Say Warwick was our anchor; what of that?
And Montague our topmast; what of him?
Our slaughter'd friends the tackles; what of these?
Why, is not Oxford here another anchor?
And Somerset another goodly mast?
The friends of France our shrouds and tacklings?
And, though unskillful, why not Ned and I
For once allow'd the skillful pilot's charge?
We will not from the helm to sit and weep,
But keep our course, though the rough wind say no,
From shelves and rocks that threaten us with wrack.
As good to chide the waves as speak them fair.
And what is Edward but a ruthless sea?
What Clarence but a quicksand of deceit?
And Richard but a ragged fatal rock?
All these the enemies to our poor bark.
Say you can swim; alas, 'tis but a while;
Tread on the sand; why, there you quickly sink:
Bestride the rock; the tide will wash you off,
Or else you famish—that's a threefold death.
This speak I, lords, to let you understand,
If case some one of you would fly from us,
That there's no hoped-for mercy with the brothers
More than with ruthless waves, with sands and rocks.
Why, courage then! What cannot be avoided
'Twere childish weakness to lament or fear.

KING RICHARD III
LADY ANNE—ACT I, SCENE 2

AGE: Young [Any age]. INTENT: Serious.

King Richard III is Shakespeare's first great play. It has been a popular stage favorite almost without interruption from the 1590s to the present day. Actors clamor to do Richard, and actresses long to play Lady Anne. It is also, with the exception of *Hamlet*, the longest of Shakespeare's plays. Richard III and Falstaff seem to have been the two favorite Shakespearean characters for the Elizabethans.

Lady Anne is the first in a line of gentle Shakespearean women who possess refined grace and fortitude and are victims of adversity that is not of their making, not within their control. Desdemona, Imogen, Hero, and Hermione are among those who trail in Lady Anne's wake.

Lady Anne has every reason to fear, to distrust, to dislike, and to mourn the actions of the Yorkists. Her father, the powerful kingmaker, the Earl of Warwick, was wounded in battle against the Yorkists, and he was left to die on the field of his wounds by the present king, Edward IV. Her husband, Edward, Prince of Wales, and her father-in-law, King Henry VI, were both murdered in cold blood with the participation of Richard. Anne is also the great-great-great granddaughter of King Edward III, so her blood is very blue and her marriage to one of the Yorkists is most desirable. Richard wants her, but for his own plans.

Anne appears in only three scenes in the play, yet she is able to capture both the imagination and the sympathy of an audience almost instantaneously. This is her first entrance in the story. She is the sole mourner for King Henry VI, and she is following his funeral bier through the streets of London. She is filled with grief, but not self-pity, for the fall of the Lancasters.

LADY ANNE

Set down, set down your honorable load—
If honor may be shrouded in a hearse—
Whilst I awhile obsequiously lament
The untimely fall of virtuous Lancaster.
Poor key-cold figure of a holy king,
Pale ashes of the house of Lancaster,
Thou bloodless remnant of that royal blood,
Be it lawful that I invocate thy ghost
To hear the lamentations of poor Anne,
Wife to thy Edward, to thy slaughter'd son,
Stabb'd by the selfsame hand that made these wounds!
Lo, in these windows that let forth thy life,
I pour the helpless balm of my poor eyes.
O, cursed be the hand that made these holes!
Cursed the heart that had the heart to do it!
Cursed the blood that let this blood from hence!
More direful hap betide that hated wretch,
That makes us wretched by the death of thee,
Than I can wish to wolves, to spiders, toads,
Or any creeping venom'd thing that lives!
If ever he have child, abortive be it,
Prodigious, and untimely brought to light,
Whose ugly and unnatural aspect
May fright the hopeful mother at the view
And that be heir to his unhappiness!
If ever he have wife, let her be made
More miserable by the death of him
Than I am made by my young lord and thee!
Come, now towards Chertsey with your holy load,
Taken from Paul's to be interred there;
And still, as you are weary of the weight,
Rest you, whiles I lament King Henry's corse.

KING RICHARD III
QUEEN MARGARET—ACT IV, SCENE 4

AGE: Mature.   INTENT: Serious.

King Richard III has finally ascended the throne. To secure it, he has killed or made to be killed his brother, the Duke of Clarence; his nephews, the young King Edward V and the young Duke of York; Lord Hastings, the Lord Chancellor; Queen Elizabeth's brother and son, Earl Rivers and Lord Grey (respectively); and Sir Thomas Vaughan—not to mention that he also killed King Henry VI and his son, Edward, Prince of Wales; and he may have had a hand in hastening the death of his other brother, King Edward IV. Since his coronation, Richard has caused his cohort in crime, the Duke of Buckingham, to go into rebellion and then to execution. Richard has also poisoned his wife, Lady Anne, so that he may marry his own child-niece, the daughter of Edward IV.

Looming ominously at the side of all this perfidy is the haggard and deposed Queen Margaret, widow of Henry VI. She is not thought much of a threat anymore because she moves freely within the palaces and among the reigning family. She is worn and pressed by her life and losses, but she has never, never lost her thirst for revenge. She is powerless now, without base or battle-axe, so she can only fight with curses pronounced on her enemies and spout Cassandra-like prophecies.

Here the old dragon joins Richard's mother, the Dowager Duchess of York, and his sister-in-law, the Dowager Queen Elizabeth, in lamenting where their family wars have delivered them and their country, whose prosperity and safety was charged to their keep.

QUEEN MARGARET

So, now prosperity begins to mellow
And drop into the rotten mouth of death.
Here in these confines slily have I lurk'd,
To watch the waning of mine enemies.
And will to France, hoping the consequence
Will prove as bitter, black, and tragical.
       [Approaching Queen Elizabeth and Duchess
       of York.]
If ancient sorrow be most reverend,
Give mine the benefit of seniory,
And let my griefs frown on the upper hand.
If sorrow can admit society.
       [Sitting down with them.]
Tell o'er your woes again by viewing mine:
I had an Edward, till a Richard kill'd him;
I had a Harry, till a Richard kill'd him;
Thou hadst an Edward, till a Richard kill'd him;
Thou hadst a Richard, till a Richard kill'd him.
Thou hadst a Clarence too, and Richard kill'd him.
From forth the kennel of thy womb hath crept
A hell-hound that doth hunt us all to death.
That dog, that had his teeth before his eyes
To worry lambs and lap their gentle blood,
The foul defacer of God's handiwork,
That excellent grand tyrant of the earth
That reigns in galled eyes of weeping souls,
Thy womb let loose, to chase us to our graves.
O upright, just, and true-disposing God,
How do I thank thee, that this carnal cur
Preys on the issue of his mother's body,
And makes her pew-fellow with others' moan!
Bear with me. I am hungry for revenge,
And now I cloy me with beholding it.
Thy Edward he is dead, that kill'd my Edward;

Thy other Edward is dead, to quit my Edward;
Young York he is but boot, because both they
Match'd not the high perfection of my loss.
Thy Clarence he is dead that stabb'd my Edward;
And the beholders of this frantic play,
The adulterate Hastings, Rivers, Vaughan, Grey,
Untimely smother'd in their dusky graves.
Richard yet lives, hell's black intelligencer,
Only reserved their factor to buy souls
And send them thither: but at hand, at hand,
Ensues his piteous and unpitied end.
Earth gapes, hell burns, fiends roar, saints pray,
To have him suddenly convey'd from hensce
Cancel his bond of life, dear God, I pray,
That I may live to say, The dog is dead!

KING RICHARD II
DUCHESS OF YORK—ACT V, SCENE 3

AGE: Mature.   INTENT: Serious.

King Richard II has been deposed as King of England. His
cousin, Henry Bolingbroke, has replaced him on the throne as
King Henry IV. Richard had to be replaced because he had
reached a point where he could not be trusted. The nobles, to
survive, had to do something. And because he was the next true
male heir in the line of succession to the throne, Bolingbroke
was the logical choice to replace Richard. Moreover, Henry
was popular with both the nobles and with the people,
something Richard was not.

The Duke of York, uncle to both Richard and Henry, has
discovered a plot to murder Henry while he's at the
tournaments at Oxford. Among the conspirators is York's only
son, the Duke of Aumerle. York supports the Crown (whoever
is wearing it), even when contrary to his personal/family
interests. He is furious at Aumerle, and without hesitation he

rides to the King to expose the plot and accuse his son of treason.

Aumerle's mother, the Duchess of York, opposes her husband's action: blood and fatherhood are thicker than treason and regicide. She urges Aumerle to speed to the King ahead of York and to crave the King's pardon even *before* York can arrive to accuse him. She then follows them both to make her own plea to the King.

The scene is the royal palace, where Henry has first been accosted by a desperate Aurmerle asking pardon for offenses unknown, which the King grants; then, by a resolute York, determined to bring his news and his accusation. And, finally, now by the distraught Duchess, who does not know what has gone on before and begs audience. She not only means to thwart her husband, but also to beseech her sovereign as a woman for a pardon for her son.

DUCHESS OF YORK

[Without]
What ho, my liege! For God's sake, let me in!
Speak with me, pity me, open the door!
A beggar begs that never begg'd before.
   [Enter Duchess]
O King, believe not this hard-hearted man!
Love loving not itself, none other can.
Sweet York, be patient. Hear me, gentle liege. [Kneels]
For ever will I walk upon my knees,
And never see day that the happy sees,
Till thou give joy; until thou bid me joy,
By pardoning Rutland, my transgressing boy.
Pleads [York] in earnest? Look upon his face.
His eyes do drop no tears, his prayers are in jest;
His words come from his mouth, ours from our breast.
He prays but faintly and would be denied;
We pray with heart and soul and all besid.

His weary joints would gladly rise, I know;
Our knees still kneel till to the ground they grow.
His prayers are full of false hypocrisy;
Ours of true zeal and deep integrity.
Our prayers do out-pray his; then let them have
That mercy which true prayer ought to have.
          Nay, do not say, "stand up."
Say "pardon" first, and afterwards "stand up."
An if I were thy nurse, thy tongue to teach,
"Pardon" should be the first word of thy speech.
I never long'd to hear a word till now;
Say "pardon," King; let pity teach thee how.
The word is short, but not so short as sweet;
No word like "pardon" for kings' mouths so meet.
Speak "pardon" as 'tis current in our land;
The chopping French we do not understand.
Thine eye begins to speak; set thy tongue there,
Or in thy piteous heart plant thou thine ear,
That hearing how our plaints and prayers do pierce,
Pity may move thee "pardon" to rehearse.
          I do not sue to stand.
Pardon is all the suit I have in hand.
O happy vantage of a kneeling knee!
Yet am I sick for fear. Speak it again;
Twice saying "pardon" doth not pardon twain,
But makes one pardon strong.
A god on earth thou art.
Come, my old son. I pray God make thee new.

KING JOHN
CONSTANCE—ACT III, SCENE 1

AGE: Any age.   INTENT: Serious.

King John is strictly an Elizabethan chronicle play; and it has
never been very popular, perhaps because of its style (which
harkens back to pageant plays and to formal tableaux). The
play, however, is peopled with dramatic and sympathetic and
sinister characters. Some of the passages are eloquently
written, stirring, and moving.

Constance is a dramatically effective character; one of
Shakespeare's most imaginative, impassioned, and eloquent
women. She is the widow of Geoffrey Plantagenet, third son of
King Henry II and younger brother of King Richard I (Coeur-
de-lion). Geoffrey pre-deceased Richard, and Richard had
named Geoffrey's son, Arthur, his heir in 1190. Before Arthur
can claim the throne on the death of his uncle, his other uncle,
and Richard's youngest brother, John, produced a later will that
named him heir before Arthur. Arthur at this time is still a
minor, so Constance is fighting for his claim—intent to use
force, if necessary, to gain England by allying herself with
France and Austria. Constance's whole life is dominated by her
love for Arthur and her ambitions for him. She is not much
principled nor does she entertain much fairness of mind when it
comes to his rights and claims to the English throne.

She is a well-developed character who progresses through
the play from a forlorned widow's state to one of apprehension,
then to states of anger and resentment as the betrayal of her son
(and herself) and his cause by the various monarchs evolves.
Constance reacts against all the "trafficking and bargaining"
with a natural resentment. Finally, she is driven crazy with
grief when Arthur falls into the hands of King John.

The powers of England and France have met before the city
of Angiers, with inconclusive results. But the truce terms are
by no means inconclusive. In return for withdrawing their

support to Arthur's claim to the English throne, John gives France his niece in marriage to the French Dauphin, Lewis, and as her dowry returns five rich French provinces. John offers as consolation to make Arthur Duke of Brittany, which he already is, and Lord of Angiers. A poor substitute for a crown and an empire.

The Earl of Salisbury has just delivered the news of the truce and the marriage to Constance and Arthur. He has also been instructed to escort them to the two kings.

CONSTANCE

Gone to be married? gone to swear peace?
False blood to false blood join'd! gone to be friends?
Shall Lewis have Blanch, and Blanch those provinces?
It is not so; thou has misspoke, misheard.
Be well advised, tell o'er thy tale again.
It cannot be; thou dost but say 'tis so.
I trust I may not trust thee, for thy word
Is but the vain breath of a common man.
Believe me, I do not believe thee, man;
I have a king's oath to the contrary.
Thou shalt be punish'd for thus frighting me,
For I am sick and capable of fears,
Oppress'd with wrongs, and therefore full of fears,
A widow, husbandless, subject to fears,
A woman, naturally born to fears;
And though thou now confess thou didst but jest,
With my vex'd spirits I cannot take a truce,
But they will quake and tremble all this day.
What dost thou mean by shaking of thy head?
Why dost thou look so sadly on my son?
What means that hand upon that breast of thine?
Why holds thy eye that lamentable rheum,
Like a proud river peering o'er his bounds?
Be these sad signs confirmers of thy words?

Then speak again—not all thy former tale,
But this one word, whether thy tale be true.
O, if thou teach me to believe this sorrow,
Teach thou this sorrow how to make me die,
And let belief and life encounter so
As doth the fury of two desperate men
Which in the very meeting fall and die.
Lewis marry Blanch! O boy, then where art thou?
France friend with England, what becomes of me?
France is a bawd to Fortune and King John,
That strumpet Fortune, that usurping John!
Tell me, thou fellow, is not France forsworn?
Envenom him with words, or get thee gone
And leave those woes alone which I alone
Am bound to underbear. I will not go with thee.
I will instruct my sorrows to be proud,
For grief is proud and makes his owner stoop.
To me and to the state of my great grief
Let kings assemble, for my grief's so great
That no supporter but the huge firm earth
Can hold it up. Here I and sorrows sit;
Here is my throne, bid kings come bow to it.

KING JOHN
CONSTANCE—ACT III, SCENE 4

AGE: Any age.   INTENT: Serious.

Right upon the heels of the newly established peace between
England and France, Pandulph, the papal legate, arrives. John
has defied the Pope by blocking the installment of Stephen
Langton as Archbishop of Canterbury. As a result, John is excommunicated. Pandulph charges France to "desert England"
and to become the "champion of our church," or France stands
to be excommunicated as well.

In the ensuing war, France loses. Arthur is captured by John
and is taken to England by force. His fate is unknown, but sus-
pected. Constance knows what will happen to her son in
England. Deserted, distraught, desperate, deranged, Constance
confronts King Philip of France, the Dauphin Lewis, and
Pandulph.

CONSTANCE

Lo, now! Now see the issue of your peace.
No, I defy all counsel, all redress,
But that which ends all counsel, true redress,
Death, death. O amiable, lovely death,
Thou odoriferous stench! Sound rottenness,
Arise forth from the couch of lasting night,
Thou hate and terror to prosperity,
And I will kiss thy detestable bones,
And put my eyeballs in thy vaulty brows,
And ring these fingers with thy household worms,
And stop this gap of breath with fulsome dust,
And be a carrion monster like thyself.
Come, grin on me, and I will think thou smil'st,
And buss thee as thy wife. Misery's love,
O, come to me!
O, that my tongue were in the thunder's mouth!
Then with a passion would I shake the world,
And rouse from sleep that fell anatomy
Which cannot hear a lady's feeble voice,
Which scorns a modern invocation.
Thou are not holy to belie me so.
I am not mad. This hair I tear is mine;
My name is Constance; I was Geoffrey's wife;
Young Arthur is my son, and he is lost.
I am not mad; I would to heaven I were!
For then, 'tis like I should forget myself.
O, if I could, what grief should I forget?

Preach some philosophy to make me mad,
And thou shall be canonized, Cardinal;
For being not mad, but sensible of grief,
My reasonable part produces reason
How I may be deliver'd of these woes,
And teaches me to kill or hang myself.
If I were mad, I should forget my son,
Or madly think a babe of clouts were he.
I am not mad. Too well, too well I feel
The different plague of each calamity.
I tore [hair] from their bonds, and cried aloud
"O that these hands could so redeem my son,
As they have given these hairs their liberty!"
But now I envy at their liberty,
And will again commit them to their bonds,
Because my poor child is a prisoner.
And, father Cardinal, I have heard you say
That we shall see and know our friends in heaven.
If that be true, I shall see my boy again;
For since the birth of Cain, the first male child,
To him that did but yesterday suspire,
There was not such a gracious creature born.
But now will canker sorrow eat my bud
And chase the native beauty from his cheek,
And he will look as hollow as a ghost,
As dim and meagre as an ague's fit,
And so he'll die; and, rising so again,
When I shall meet him in the court of heaven
I shall not know him. Therefore never, never
Must I behold my pretty Arthur more.
Grief fills the room up of my absent child,
Lies in his bed, walks up and down with me,
Puts on his pretty looks, repeats his words,
Remembers me of all his gracious parts,
Stuffs out his vacant garments with his form;
Then, have I reason to be fond of grief?

Fare you well! Had you such a loss as I,
I could give better comfort than you do.
I will not keep this form upon my head,
When there is such disorder in my wit.
O Lord! My boy, my Arthur, my fair son!
My life, my joy, my food, my all the world!
My widow-comfort, and my sorrows' cure!
      [Exit]

KING HENRY IV, PART I
LADY PERCY—ACT II, SCENE 3

AGE: Any age [Young].   INTENT: Serious.

The two *King Henry IV* plays are enshrined for their greatest comic creation, Sir John Falstaff, that grand progenitor of numerous humorous types that now abound in dramatic literature. But while the *Henry* plays abound with masculine types, Shakespeare uses the women of the play to humanize the soldier/hero and the braggarts. Lady Percy's brief span upon the stage is an apogee of this use.

Lord Henry Percy, surnamed "Hotspur," is a gallant and brave soldier and a man of honor and honesty, but he is also hot-headed and will jump to action no matter what the consequences. The Percys aided King Henry in his rebellion against King Richard II and had helped Henry gain the crown. Now, they feel they are misused and under-appreciated by the new monarch. Moreover, Hotspur had learned that his brother-in-law, Mortimer, the Earl of March, had been named by Richard II as his heir to the throne. So, Hotspur might have done his own kinsman an injustice by aiding Henry. Hotspur is in a quandary, and he is being pressured to join forces with the Welsh in open rebellion against the king.

Lady Percy is devoted to Hotspur. She is also a wife in whom her husband mostly confides: they are friends as well as lovers. But now Hotspur is acting uncharacteristically toward her. He has closed her off, is restless, his sleep troubled with dreams, and he has abandoned their bed. Lady Percy is worried, and she wants Hotspur to reveal his disquiet to her.

LADY PERCY

O, my good lord, why are you thus alone?
For what offense have I this fortnight been
A banish'd woman from my Harry's bed?
Tell me, sweet lord, what is 't that takes from thee
Thy stomach, pleasure, and thy golden sleep?
Why dost thou bend thine eyes upon the earth,
And start so often when thou sit'st alone?
Why hast thou lost the fresh blood in thy cheeks,
And given my treasures and my rights of thee
To thick-eyed musing and curs'd melancholy?
In thy faint slumbers I by thee have watch'd,
And heard thee murmur tales of iron wars,
Speak terms of manage to thy bounding steed,
Cry, "Courage! To the field!" And thou hast talk'd
Of sallies and retires, of trenches, tents,
Of palisadoes, frontiers, parapets,
Of basilisks, of cannon, culverin,
Of prisoners' ransom, and of soldiers slain,
And all the currents of a heady fight.
Thy spirit within thee hath been so at war,
And thus hath so bestirr'd thee in thy sleep,
That beads of sweat have stood upon thy brow
Like bubbles in a late-disturbed stream,
And in thy face strange motions have appear'd,
Such as we see when men restrain their breath
On some great sudden hest. O, what portents are these?
Some heavy business hath my lord in hand,
And I must know it, else he loves me not.